A PARENT'S SURVIVAL GUIDE TO PHONICS AND SPELLING

Help your child through the phonics maze!

ANDREW BRODIE

Published 2011 by A&C Black Publishers Limited
36 Soho Square, London W1D 3QY
www.acblack.com

ISBN 978-1-4081-407-41

Text © Andrew Brodie 2011
Photographs © Fotolia, © Shutterstock
Design by Lynda Murray

Cover photographs © Shutterstock

The writer and publishers gratefully acknowledge reference to the document
'Letters and Sounds: Principles and Practice of High Quality Phonics', Crown
Copyright 2007

Printed in Great Britain by Martins the Printers, Berwick-upon-Tweed

This book is produced using paper that is made from wood grown in
managed, sustainable forests. It is natural, renewable and recyclable.
The logging and manufacturing processes conform to the environmental
regulations of the country of origin.

To see our full range of titles
visit www.acblack.com

Contents

❓ Why do you need this book?

In recent years, children have been encouraged to learn how to read and spell using a method called 'synthetic phonics'. Through this approach the children learn how sounds are synthesised (blended together) for reading words.

This book will explain exactly what learning through phonics means. It will tell you all you need to know about the programme of work your child is working through at school. You will soon learn, for example, about the 'six phases' of the teaching programme and you will be able to identify which phase your child is currently following. This book will help to reveal the mysteries behind terms such as 'phonemes' and 'graphemes' and will show you how phonics may be used to teach spelling as well as reading.

Is this a familiar scene in your home?

Helping your children to read is one of the most useful things you can do for them. It will help them to gain confidence with their learning in many other subjects in school and will be a great step-up into life beyond school. In this book you will find 'handy tips' and 'quick ideas' for activities that you can easily share with your child at home.

❓ What happens when?

The process of learning to spell tends to follow on from learning to read but again there are clear steps to follow at each stage of your child's development. Learning to spell well will help your child with all aspects of writing across all curriculum areas. The guidance in this book will help you to support your child's progress in spelling. Near the back of the book there are lists of words that you can practise with your child to help them become an accurate and confident speller.

The book is invaluable for parents of children at Key Stage 1, but is also suitable for those with older children who need to build their confidence.

What if my child is dyslexic?

Evidence suggests that a systematic approach to phonics when learning to read and write can be very effective for children with dyslexia. Using the activities in this book, alongside the work your child experiences at school, will help your child to make progress.

What happens in school?

Primary education is separated into three phases: Early Years Foundation Stage, Key Stage 1 and Key Stage 2. You can see at a glance how your child fits into each phase in this chart.

Foundation Stage	Reception	Up to age 5
Key Stage 1	Year 1	Age 5-6
	Year 2	Age 6-7
Key Stage 2	Year 3	Age 7-8
	Year 4	Age 8-9
	Year 5	Age 9-10
	Year 6	Age 10-11

The *Letters and Sounds* programme

In school, your child will follow a programme of learning to read and spell called *Letters and Sounds*. It is organised into six phases (see pages 8-9). Phases One to Four take place in the Reception class and help children to learn all the letters of the alphabet and start to read simple words. Phase Five builds on this throughout Year 1 and Phase Six is taught throughout Year 2.

What happens after the six phases are completed?

The teaching and learning process continues long after the *Letters and Sounds* programme has been taught. Your child will be given a wider and wider range of reading materials. They will be encouraged to read for information and pleasure and will learn to search texts for meaning. As the process of learning to spell is often developed later than reading, your child will continue to learn the spelling of individual words, identifying spelling patterns that follow known patterns and learning new words that feature exceptions to normal 'rules'.

Jargon-busting guide

Phonics	Method of teaching children to read and write. It shows children that the sounds in our language are represented by letters or groups of letters.
Phonemes	There are 26 letters in our alphabet and these can be combined together to represent the sounds that we use in speaking. These sounds are known as phonemes.
Synthetic phonics	Reading words consists of blending together the sounds (phonemes) represented by the letters in each word – so 'synthetic phonics' is all about synthesising the phonemes in words.
Blending	The skill of putting together the individual sounds that make up a word.
Graphemes	A letter, or a group of letters, that make up a sound.
Decode	The ability to read a word by saying the individual sounds and then blending them together.
Segmenting	The skill of breaking a word down into its various sounds. This makes the word easier to spell.
Syllables	These are the number of beats in each word. So, picture has two syllables pic-ture and computer has three com-pu-ter.
Alliteration	Where two or more words begin with the same letter or sound, such as the 'green grass is growing'.

For more details see 'Useful information' on page 95.

The six phases of *Letters and Sounds*

Here's a handy guide to the six phases of learning to read through synthetic phonics.

Phase One

Your child is introduced to blending phonemes (the sounds represented by letters) together to make whole words by listening to an adult and copying the sounds. At this stage they won't look at the letters themselves but will listen to the sounds that the letters represent.

 Although there are 26 letters of the alphabet, we speak our words by using 44 different sounds (phonemes). The children will be taught about 42 phonemes.

 Your child will be taught very pure sounds. So, for example, the phoneme /**n**/ will be pronounced **nnnnnnnn**, not **nuh**.

 Phonemes can be represented by writing the letters between two forward slashes. For example the letters **s** and **h** in the word ship make the sound /**sh**/. The children will not be shown this method of writing the phonemes but if you ever come across it, this is what it's for!

Phase Two

Your child will be introduced to systematic learning through phonics and 'grapheme-phoneme correspondences'. These are the link between written letters and the sounds that they represent. The children are taught to 'decode' the words to read them by building them up from sounds and letters. Reading is taught through **blending** separate phonemes to make whole words. Spelling is taught through **segmenting** whole words into their individual phonemes.

 Individual letters and combinations of letters written down that represent phonemes are known as graphemes. For example, the phoneme /**s**/ is normally represented by the grapheme **s** and the phoneme /**ai**/ is normally represented by the grapheme **ay** (as in **day**) or **ai** (as in **pain**).

Phase Three

Your child will complete their learning of the alphabet and will now look at sounds represented by more than one letter, for example, the sound made by the two letters **s** and **h** together: /**sh**/. Note that sh is a single grapheme as it makes one phoneme (sound).

Phase Four

Your child will experience reading and spelling words containing adjacent consonants (any letter which is not a vowel). They will practise words such as 'stop', where the two separate sounds made by the letters **s** and **t** are blended together to say **st**.

Phase Five

Your child will learn a wider range of graphemes and phonemes. They will continue to discover that some graphemes have alternative pronunciations and that some phonemes can be represented by more than one grapheme.

handy tip

Your child will learn that the grapheme **ow** represents a different sound in **now** to the sound it makes in **snow** and they will learn that the phoneme /**ee**/ appears with different graphemes in words such as s**ee**, s**ea**, k**ey**, bab**y**.

Phase Six

Your child will be encouraged to become a fluent reader and to gain increasing accuracy in their spelling. By now they will know most of the grapheme-phoneme correspondences.

At Phase Six most children are able to read a very large number of words and will be increasing their vocabulary all the time. They should now have the skills to decode words very quickly because they are so good at blending sounds together. They will be learning to spell an ever wider range of words.

handy tip

When talking to you as a parent the teachers may refer to grapheme-phoneme correspondences. These are the direct links between the letters (graphemes) and the sounds (phonemes) they represent.

Vowel sounds

Five of the letters of the alphabet are vowels: **a e i o u**. Nearly every word in the English language contains at least one vowel, as it's so difficult to say a syllable without a vowel in it. The list below shows the vowel phonemes (sounds) and gives some examples of words that contain these. Some of the examples can be quite surprising: it seems strange that the letter **e** can say /**i**/ but it does in the words planted or repeat.

handy tip

People in some parts of the country use different phonemes for the same word. For example, some people in some regions say the sound /**a**/ in the word path whereas others will say the sound /**ar**/.

Vowel phonemes	Sample words
/a/	bat
/e/	leg, guess, head, said, says
/i/	big, planted, busy, crystal, decide, exact, guilt, repeat
/o/	dog, honest, was, quarrel, trough, vault, yacht *(the ch is silent)*
/u/	bug, love, blood, comfort, rough, would, young
/ae/	rain, day, game, navy, weigh, they, great, rein
/ee/	been, team, field, these, he, key, litre, quay, suite
/ie/	pie, high, sign, my, bite, child, guide, guy, haiku
/oe/	boat, goes, crow, cone, gold, sew
/ue/ (/oo/)	soon, do, July, blue, chew, June, bruise, shoe, you, move, through

Vowel phonemes	Sample words
/oo/	book, could, foot
/ar/	barn, bath *(regional)*, laugh *(regional)*, baa, half, clerk, heart, guard
/ur/	Thursday, girl *(regional)*, her, learn, word
/or/	born, door, warm, all, draw, cause, talk, aboard, abroad, before, four, bought, taught
/ow/	brown, found, plough
/oi/	join, toy, buoy
/air/	chair, pear, care, where, their, prayer
/ear/	near, cheer, here, weird, pier

Try saying this vowel phoneme:

/er/	faster, gazump, currant, woollen, circus

Not to be confused with the phoneme /**ur**/, this phoneme is very similar to /**u**/ but is slightly different in some regions.

Consonant sounds

The letters that are not vowels are consonants. We tend to pronounce consonants by putting our lips together or by using our tongue or our teeth. Try each of the consonant phonemes and observe what you do!

handy tip

We don't expect children to learn tricky words such as psalm at this stage but they are shown on the list below as examples of how the phonemes might appear in written words.

Consonant phonemes	Sample words	Consonant phonemes	Sample words
/b/	**b**ag	/s/	**c**inema, goo**s**e, li**s**ten, **ps**alm, **sc**ene, **s**ee, **s**word
/d/	**d**ad, coul**d**	/t/	**t**en, recei**pt**
/f/	cal**f**, **f**ast, gra**ph**, tou**gh**	/v/	**v**est
/g/	**gh**ost, **g**irl	/w/	**w**et
/h/	**h**ere, **wh**o	/wh/	**wh**en (regional)
/j/	bri**dg**e, **g**iraffe, hu**g**e, **j**et	/y/	**y**es
/k/	anti**qu**e, **c**at, loo**k**, **qu**iet, **ch**oir, si**x** *(note that the sound made by the letter **x** is a blend of the phonemes /**k**/ and /**s**/)*	/z/	choo**s**e, wa**s**, **z**oo
/l/	**l**eg	/th/	**th**e
/m/	**m**ug, cli**mb**, autu**mn**	/th/	**th**ank
/n/	**n**ow, **gn**ash, **kn**ight, si**gn**	/ch/	**ch**eer, ma**tch**
/p/	**p**eg	/sh/	**sh**op, se**ss**ion, **ch**ute
/r/	**r**un, **r**ain, **wr**ote	/zh/	u**s**ual
		/ng/	thi**ng**, thi**n**k

Phase One takes place in the Reception class (ages four to five). It presents an exciting start to learning about sounds. Your child will be encouraged to develop their speaking and listening skills to prepare them fully for starting to read and write.

Talk, talk, talk!
Take every opportunity to talk to your child. Tell them about what you're doing, where you're going, where you've been, what you can see out of the window – in fact, anything that can be talked about.

Talk about pictures in a magazine. What can you see in the picture? What different colours can you see?

What can you see out of the window? Can you see any trees, flowers, houses, birds or cars? Ask your child to describe what they can see in as much detail as possible. Give lots of praise for each observation. What do they notice that they've never noticed before?

Listen, listen, listen!
Take every opportunity to listen to your child. Ask them to tell you about what they are doing, what they have done at school, who they played with — in fact, anything that can be talked about. Of course, they are likely to say 'not much'. Try telling them about your day — they're more likely to tell you about theirs!

handy tip

What did you do at school today?

Not much.

Event swapping!
Tell your child what you did before your coffee break. Can your child remember what they did before break?

Tell your child what you had for lunch. Can your child remember what they had?

Tell your child what you did in the afternoon. Can your child describe their afternoon?

If your child doesn't remember anything, don't worry! At least they have listened to your descriptions and may remember more the following day.

quick idea

The seven aspects of learning

Phase One activities are organised as seven aspects of learning about sounds.

Aspect 1

Environmental sounds

Your child will be encouraged to listen and to describe what they can hear indoors or outdoors to encourage their general sound discrimination.

Aspect 2

Instrumental sounds

What sounds do different instruments make? Can your child distinguish between sounds made by shakers, drums, guitar strings?

Aspect 3

Body percussion

To continue their exploration of general sound discrimination your child will perform sounds and actions such as clapping, stamping or patting their knees in time with a song or rhyme.

Aspect 4

Rhythm and rhyme

Your child will listen to and join in with a wide variety of rhymes, including nursery rhymes and rhyming books.

Aspect 5

Alliteration

Identifying the opening sounds of different words is a very important aid to developing the skills needed for reading. Your child will enjoy playing with words that start with the same sound.

Claire is **c**uddling a **c**at

Aspect 6

Voice sounds

Is your child aware of how many different sounds they can make with their mouths?! Can they make the buzzing sound of a bee? Can they moo like a cow? Can they neigh like a horse?

neighhhhh!

Aspect 7

Oral blending and segmenting

Your child will begin to learn about phonemes. The teacher will choose some short single-syllable words to segment into separate phonemes then blend them back together. For example, the teacher may show a picture of a dog and say 'Look at the **d-o-g**, **dog**.' Note that the teacher will only segment the last word in a sentence and not words that occur at the beginning or anywhere in the middle.

handy tip

Your child should hear very pure sounds. So, for example, when listening to the phoneme /**m**/ they should hear **mmmmmm**, not **muh**.

Aspect 1
Environmental sounds

Your child will be given a wide range of experiences to help them to recognise and tell different sounds apart. Look at what your child's teacher does – there are great opportunities to do similar activities at home.

Listening walks

The class might take walks within the school or beyond. At certain points, the children will be asked to be 'good listeners' by keeping quiet and having their ears and their eyes ready. What can they hear? When they return to their class they will be asked to remember what they heard. The teacher may have made recordings of some of the sounds to replay them to the children.

Take your child for a walk in your own garden or street. Encourage your child to distinguish between different sounds – can they hear birds, cars, lorries, insects? If necessary, give some suggestions. After a while they won't need these clues.

Listening moments

These may happen at any time during the school day. Your child's teacher will ask the children to listen for perhaps 30 seconds, then to describe what they have heard and to try to identify what made the sound.

What can you hear?
This is a game that can be played any time and any place. Ask your child what they can hear. Can they hear a television on, someone talking in another room, keys being pressed on a computer keyboard, a kettle boiling?

Drumming, tapping, stroking

In class each child will be given a wooden beater and asked to try making different sounds on different objects in their outdoor area, such as fences, pipes, pots. They will be challenged to play the sounds loudly and softly.

 Give your child a wooden spoon then go outside and listen to the different sounds that can be made. What sound does a watering can make when beaten? How about a wall when the spoon is scraped along it? Which of the sounds can be made softly? Which ones can be played loudly?

Talking about sounds

As with all of the activities in school, the children will be encouraged to listen and to talk. They will, for example, hear the sounds made by familiar objects such as bunches of keys, crisp packets, rice in plastic containers, then they will be asked to identify the objects or perhaps to describe or imitate the sounds they've heard. They may hear the sounds made by pebbles or shells contained in a sock, then talk about the seaside.

 Before you start, make sure that all bottles and packages are well sealed! Ask your child to find items in your food cupboard that can be used to make sounds. They could try shaking non–fizzy liquid in a plastic bottle or peanuts in a pot. They could rustle a crisp packet or the wrapper on a bag of potatoes. After trying several sounds, ask them to turn their back while you repeat the sounds – can they tell you what made each sound?

All of these activities are designed to 'train your child's ear'. Telling different sounds apart is an important step towards making the fine distinctions between different letter sounds in words. It seems amazing that helping your child to tell the difference between the sounds made by peanuts or by rice grains in a pot may actually help them with reading and spelling, but it's true!

17

Aspect 2
Instrumental sounds

At school your child will be given a wide range of experiences to help them to tell sounds apart. They will sing songs and accompany them with percussion instruments. Look at what your child's teacher does – there are great opportunities to do similar activities at home.

Sing, sing, sing!

Your child will sing lots of songs in school. Many of these will be very well-known traditional songs and sometimes the teachers and the children themselves will make up new words to them.

Choose a familiar song, such as 'Old Macdonald Had a Farm', and help your child to make up some new words using names and sounds of family members or favourite toys. For example, if you have a baby girl:

'Old Macdonald had a house,
ee–i–ee–i–o!
And in that house, there lived young Sophie, ee–i–ee–i–o!
With a yell, yell, here and a yell, yell, there
Here a yell, there a yell, everywhere a yell, yell.'
    Old Macdonald had a house,
    ee–i–ee–i–o!'

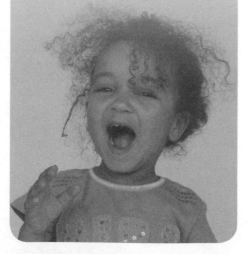

Listen to instruments

At school your child will have the opportunity to play different percussion instruments. They will be encouraged to distinguish between the sounds they make. Once they're familiar with them, the instruments will be used for accompanying songs and rhymes.

Make some shakers using small plastic milk cartons containing different items such as lentils, rice, raisins, sand and small stones. Encourage your child to try out each shaker, perhaps to accompany the rhythm of a nursery rhyme. Now ask them to look away while you rattle one of the shakers – can they tell which one it is?

Matching sound patterns

In class the children may be asked to sit in a small group while one child makes a sound with one of the instruments. Each of the others has to copy the sound as closely as possible. With further practice, a pattern of sounds will be introduced.

quick idea Ask your child to copy sounds that you make with your home-made shaker. Can they copy the pattern of sounds?

Sounds in stories

Your child's teacher will encourage them to create appropriate sound effects for stories. For example, they might use their percussion instruments to make the sounds of the Very Hungry Caterpillar crunching its food.

quick idea Use your home-made instruments to create sound effects for stories that you read to your child. This might seem very difficult to do but try it for every book that you share and the ideas will begin to flow!

Talk, talk, talk!

As always, your child will be encouraged to talk about their experiences with the sounds they make with the instruments. They will be learning new words by describing the sounds as **loud**, **quiet**, **bumpy**, **wobbly**, **squeaky** and so on.

handy tip Is your child hearing all sounds clearly? If you have any doubts about your child's hearing have it checked by your health visitor or doctor.

Aspect 3
Body percussion

Aspect 3 features further activities to help your child to discriminate between sounds. They will sing songs and accompany them with body percussion sounds, such as claps, stamps and knee pats. Look at what your child's teacher does – there are great opportunities to do similar activities at home.

Action songs

Singing songs will be an everyday activity in most Reception classrooms. There will be a variety of songs, including nursery rhymes, and your child will be encouraged to add body percussion sounds in time to the beat. They will change the body sounds with each line of the song and they will be taught to move in time with the song. They will learn that sometimes they need to add sounds, sometimes they need to move and sometimes they need to be still.

 Find a book of nursery rhymes, perhaps with an accompanying CD.

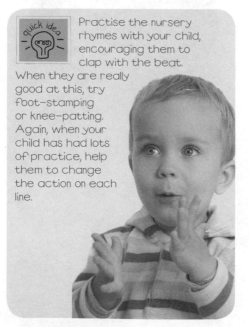

Practise the nursery rhymes with your child, encouraging them to clap with the beat. When they are really good at this, try foot-stamping or knee-patting. Again, when your child has had lots of practice, help them to change the action on each line.

Checking progress

Your child's teacher will be constantly monitoring all the children's progress, checking whether they join in with words and actions, whether they keep in time with the beat and whether they articulate the words clearly. They will also want to know if each child is producing contrasts in rhythm, speed and volume, copying sounds and making up patterns of sound.

 Ask your child to clap in time with your clapping. Try slow claps and fast claps. Can your child keep time with you? Try varying the beat: three slow claps, three fast claps – keep repeating this. Can your child join in as you clap?

Move to the beat

At school, your child will be encouraged to move in different ways, perhaps with a particular beat. They will try movements such as slow walking, fast walking, marching, hopping and skipping.

Talk, talk, talk!

Once again, your child will be given lots of opportunities to talk. Their teacher will ask them when it's a good time to be quiet and when it's a good time to be noisy!

Ask your child whether it's time to be quiet or to be noisy when they are:

- in bed
- playing in the garden
- watching television
- eating a meal
- in the park
- at the seaside.

Find any piece of music that has a clear and regular beat. Use very simple repeating dance steps that follow the beat, encouraging your child to join in.

Help your child to use the correct vocabulary when talking about sounds. Do they use words such as **quiet** and **loud**, **slow** and **fast**, **long** and **short**, **beat**?

hop

jump

skip

21

Aspect 4
Rhythm and rhyme

Every day at school your child will enjoy the experience of hearing their teacher reading rhyming stories and poems. They will join in with any repetitive phrases, copying their teacher in saying these with lots of expression. The teacher will use a variety of books, from those containing traditional nursery rhymes to modern books such as *The Gruffalo* by Julia Donaldson and Axel Scheffler (Macmillan Children's Books).

Feel the beat!

Once again, your child will use percussion instruments and body percussion in school to play rhythms that match those in the stories and rhymes that they are enjoying. They will use a variety of movements in time to the beat.

 Choose any nursery rhyme to sing or say with your child, encouraging them to join in with the repetition. Can you make up actions together? Use the nursery rhymes from pages 24 and 25.

 Look through the books that you have at home. Which ones feature rhyme? Books such as 'Monkey and Me' by Emily Gravett (Macmillan Children's Books) and 'We're Going on a Bear Hunt' by Michael Rosen and Helen Oxenbury (Walker Books Ltd) also feature lots of repetition that your child can join in with. Read a different book every day, returning to favourite ones regularly.

 Make two shakers by part-filling plastic containers with grains of rice or lentils. With your child, shake the instruments to the beat of a song on a radio. Try shaking to the rhythm of a favourite nursery rhyme.

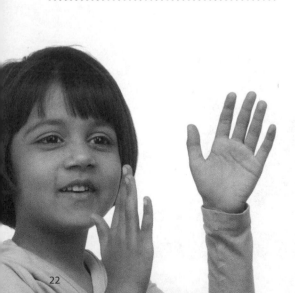

Rhyme time

As they move towards looking at words at school, your child will begin to develop skills in finding words that rhyme. They will be shown pictures of objects and will be asked to find pictures of other objects with names that rhyme.

quick idea

Use the pictures on pages 26 and 27 to encourage your child to find pictures of objects with names that rhyme. Can they find the pairs of objects? Can they find the one set of objects that has more than two members?

Aspect 4: Favourite rhymes

London Bridge

London Bridge is falling down,
Falling down, falling down,
London Bridge is falling down,
My fair Lady.

Build it up with wood and clay,
Wood and clay, wood and clay,
Build it up with wood and clay,
My fair Lady.

Wood and clay will wash away,
Wash away, wash away,
Wood and clay will wash away,
My fair Lady.

Build it up with bricks and mortar,
Bricks and mortar, bricks and mortar,
Build it up with bricks and mortar,
My fair Lady.

Hey Diddle, Diddle!

Hey Diddle, Diddle!
The cat and the fiddle,
The cow jumped over the moon.
The little dog laughed to see such fun,
And the dish ran away with the spoon.

Humpty Dumpty

Humpty Dumpty sat on a wall,
Humpty Dumpty had a great fall.
All the King's horses
And all the King's men
Couldn't put Humpty together again.

Incy Wincy Spider

Incy Wincy spider climbed up the water spout,

Down came the rain and washed poor Incy out,

Out came the sunshine and dried up all the rain,

And Incy Wincy spider climbed up the spout again.

Sing a Song of Sixpence

Sing a song of sixpence,

A pocket full of rye;

Four and twenty blackbirds

Baked in a pie.

When the pie was opened,

The birds began to sing;

Wasn't that a dainty dish

To set before the king?

The King was in his counting-house,

Counting out his money;

The Queen was in her parlour

Eating bread and honey;

The maid was in the garden

Hanging out the clothes,

When down came a black-bird

And pecked off her nose!

25

Aspect 4: Find the rhymes

27

Words and syllables

As part of Aspect 4 your child will begin to investigate the syllable patterns of words that have two or more syllables. The teacher will discuss everyday objects with the children, then talk about the sounds in the names of these objects. They will ask the children to clap out the syllables as they say each word.

Syllables are the number of beats in each word. So, pencil has two syllables **pen-cil** and elephant has three, **el-e-phant**.

Try the words listed below. Show your child the objects rather than the words. Talk about the words, then help your child to break each word into its syllables.

window

computer

helicopter

table

aeroplane

Aspect 5
Alliteration

Word play will be a regular feature of classroom life. At this stage, your child will experience lots of activities concentrating on the initial sounds of words.

Alliteration is where two or more words begin with the same letter or sound, such as **Suzy sang a sweet song**.

What's your name?

They are likely to start with the initial sounds of their own names, playing games such as 'I spy someone whose name begins with...' then moving on to short simple tongue twisters made up on the spot: Tom's table is tidy, Maddie's mug is marvellous.

quick idea

Use your own child's name for making short tongue twisters: Ben's a big boy, Molly's made a mess! The words don't have to make complete sense in themselves – they don't have to form a sentence but can simply be an alliterative phrase, such as **Jack's jolly jelly**.

Treasure hunt

At school your child will play games such as 'digging for treasure', where they search for objects that the teacher has hidden in the sand tray. The objects will all have the same initial letter.

quick idea

Look through the items in your fridge or kitchen cupboard. Can you find things with the same initial letter? For example, jelly, jam, juice; milk, marmite, mint; bread, biscuits, banana; cake, cookies, custard. Put out two or three items with the same initial sound and talk about them with your child, making sure that your child hears you stressing these sounds.

Checking progress

Your child's teacher will be constantly monitoring their progress, checking whether they can remember the lists of objects that started with the same sounds, whether they can discriminate between sounds and say them clearly and whether they can think of other words that start with the same sound.

Aspect 6
Voice sounds

Don't be surprised if your child comes home and does strange things with their mouth! At school they will be encouraged to blow and suck and to stretch and wiggle their tongues, perhaps practising in time with music. They will make lots of different sounds with their voices, such as mooing like a cow, stressing the **'m'** sound and extending the **'oo'** sound.

Who's speaking?

Your child's teacher may make sound recordings of the children speaking, then play them back to the children themselves or to the whole class, asking the children if they can identify each other by the sounds of their voices.

Over a period of time record the voice of each member of your family, including grandparents, brothers, sisters, aunts and uncles. Ask each person to send a message to your child. Play back each message and see if your child can identify the different people by their voices alone.

30

quick idea

Pick a favourite book that your child likes to hear you read. Read the book to your child, emphasising different voices for the characters and introducing sounds wherever possible. Can your child copy the sounds?

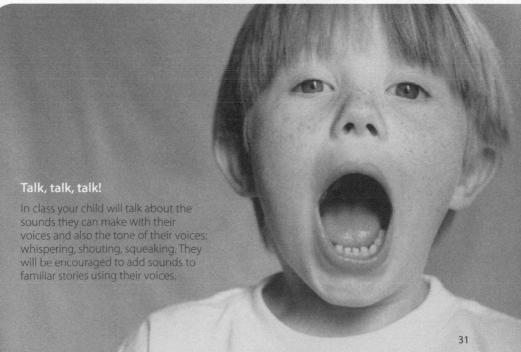

Talk, talk, talk!

In class your child will talk about the sounds they can make with their voices and also the tone of their voices: whispering, shouting, squeaking. They will be encouraged to add sounds to familiar stories using their voices.

Aspect 7
Oral blending and segmenting

At this stage your child will begin to learn about phonemes. Their teacher will choose some short single-syllable words to segment into separate phonemes then blend them back together. For example, the teacher may show a picture of a dog and say 'Look at the /**d**/-/**o**/-/**g**/, **dog**'. The teacher will only segment the last word in a sentence and not words that occur at the beginning or anywhere in the middle.

Again, nursery rhymes may provide the stimulus for some of the blending and segmenting. For example, 'Jack and Jill went up the /**h**/-/**i**/-/**l**/, **hill**'.

Some CVC (Consonant, Vowel, Consonant) words will be used as the focus for blending. Words such as **pin** will be sounded out, /**p**/-/**i**/-/**n**/, accompanied by a clap for each phoneme, then the sounds will be blended to make the whole word.

The first letters your child will meet when they start Phase 2, will be

s, a, t, p then **i, n, m** and **d**.

In this final aspect of Phase 1, the letters

s, a, t, p, i and **n**

will be combined to make words for sounding out and blending:

sat,	**sip,**
tap,	**pit,**
tip,	**pip,**
pin,	**tin,**
nip,	**tan** and so on.

handy tip

CVC words are words that are made from three sounds: an initial consonant phoneme, a central vowel phoneme and a final consonant phoneme. for example, **cat** is made from the phonemes /**c**/, /**a**/ and /**t**/. A word such as **shop** is also regarded as a CVC word – even though it starts with two consonants, as those two consonants are combined to make a single phoneme /**sh**/.

quick idea

Think of some CVC words that you can discuss with your child. Sound each word out. For example, use the word **tin**. Show your child a tin from the kitchen cupboard. Say '**tin**, /**t**/–/**i**/–/**n**/ (clapping on each phoneme), **tin**.'

'Sound-talking'

Your child's teacher will find some objects and toys with names that have three phonemes and will use a 'sound-talk' toy to demonstrate saying the names. This will be a toy rather than a puppet so that the children watch the teacher's mouth, not the mouth of a puppet. For example the toy will say /**c**/-/**a**/-/**t**/ instead of **cat**, then the children will put the sounds together to say the word. The children will repeat the sounds and blend them together.

handy tip

Here are some CVC words that can be said in sound-talk: **cat**, **dog**, **cup**, **mug**, **pot**, **bag**, **head**, **neck**, **feet**.

Segmenting

So far, your child will have been practising blending – putting together sounds to make a word. Next they will be trying to segment orally, where they separate words into 'sound-talk'. They will be copying the process that the sound-talk toy uses when saying the name of objects. For example, they may be asked to sound-talk the name of an object such as a mug. They will say /**m**/-/**u**/-/**g**/ and the other children will have to blend the phonemes to say the name of the object.

Phase Two introduces systematic learning through phonics and first shows children the 'grapheme-phoneme correspondences', ie the link between written letters and the sounds that they represent.

Week 1

When your child is ready they will move on to Phase Two of the *Letters and Sounds* programme. Now they will be using written letters and words much more. In the first week of Phase Two, your child will work on the Set 1 letters:

s a t p

 Your child won't learn the letters in the order of the alphabet but instead in sets that work well together.

Your child will learn each of the letters in turn. For each letter there will be several activities. For example, they will learn to match the letter **s** to a picture of a snake and they will say the word **snake**, stressing the /**s**/ phoneme: **sssssnake**. They will weave their hands to show how a snake moves, making an **s** shape as they do so.

The children will see a picture of a snake on a card and they will say sssssnake.

*On the other side of the card will be just the letter **s**.*

 Make four simple flashcards showing a picture on one side and a letter on the other side. Try a picture of a sock (with the letter **s** on the reverse); an ant (with **a** on the reverse); a tap (with **t** on the reverse) and a pot (with **p** on the reverse). Show your child just one card at a time. Help them to say the sound shown on the card, and to say the name of the object on the reverse. Say each letter sound as clearly and purely as possible. For example, say '**sssssss**' and not '**suh**'.

Reading practice

At this stage, your child may not be asked to learn whole words. Instead, they will be encouraged to say the correct sound when they are shown a letter.

 Using just the four letter flashcards that you have made, ask your child to make the correct sound as you show each letter in turn. Don't worry if they can't remember to start with because you can simply turn the card over and stress the letter sound as you show the picture. Spend just a few minutes on this then return to the activity the next day. Remember, practice makes perfect!

Talk to the teacher

Ask your child's teacher how you can help at home. For example, the teacher may prefer you to use cards with pictures of the same animals and objects that are used in school.

Spelling practice

Now, in school, your child will be shown all of the Set 1 letters and asked to pick out the correct letter when a sound is spoken. This is an early stage in spelling but at this point your child will not be asked to spell a word! Learning the skill of quickly identifying letters that represent sounds is a great step towards spelling success.

 Put out the four letter cards in front of your child and make one of the sounds: /s/ or /a/ or /t/ or /p/. Can your child find the correct letter for the sound? Repeat for each of the sounds. Spend just a short time on this each day.

Week 2

In the second week of Phase Two, your child will work on the Set 2 letters:

i n m d

In class, your child will practise the letters from week 1 – **s**, **a**, **t** and **p** – revising oral blending and segmentation. With the new letters they will practise blending for reading and will work on the high frequency words **is**, **it**, **in** and **at**.

handy tip

Research has shown that some words appear much more often than others in reading materials – these words are known as 'high frequency words' (see www. highfrequencywords.org). For example, the word **the** appears more than any other word. Unfortunately **the** is not easy to decode using phonic rules. During Phase Two the children will be introduced to lots of decodable high frequency words, such as **is**, **it**, **in** and **at**, and they will also meet the **tricky** words **the**, **to**, **I**, **no**, **go** and **into**.

Letter fans

As part of the initial stages of learning to spell, your child will be asked to find the correct letter when the teacher says a letter sound. They will be given letter fans showing some of the letters that they have been practising.

When the teacher says a letter sound, the children have to find the appropriate letter on their letter fan. They will separate this letter out clearly from the other letters and hold it up to show the teacher.

Week 3

In the third week of Phase Two, your child will be working on the Set 3 letters:

g o c k

Your child will practise the letters from weeks 1 and 2 – **s**, **a**, **t**, **p**, **i**, **n**, **m** and **d** – revising oral blending and segmentation. With the new letters they will practise blending for reading and will work on the word **and**.

quick idea

Write four of the letters that have been used so far on separate blank cards. Ask your child to point to the correct letter when you say one of the letter sounds. If they are correct give them the card then try one of the other letter sounds. Keep going until they have all the cards, then give lots of praise for success. If they find it difficult, start with just two cards and give lots of help. Don't forget to say each letter sound as clearly and purely as possible. For example, say '**nnnnnnnn**' and not '**nuh**'.

handy tip

The letter sound for **a** should be the sound that the letter **a** makes in the word cat and the letter sound for **o** should be the sound that the letter **o** makes in the word **cot**.

Week 4

In the fourth week of Phase Two, your child will be working on the Set 4 letters:

ck e u r

Notice that your child has already learnt the letters **c** and **k** separately and is now learning

them combined together, as they appear at the ends of words such as **sock** and **duck**.

Your child will practise the letters from the previous weeks, revising oral blending and segmentation. With the new letters they will practise blending for reading and will work on the high frequency words **to** and **the**.

Matching words and pictures

One of the many activities that your child will enjoy at school will be a matching game for words and pictures. They will have a set of picture cards and a set of corresponding word cards. For example, they may have a set of cards related to the grapheme **ck**:

rock

duck   kick

sock

sack

Short captions will also be used as reading practice:

a duck and a sock

Week 5

At this stage your child will work on the Set 5 letters. This includes the introduction to double letters.

h b f ff l ll ss

Your child will practise the letters from the previous weeks, revising oral blending and segmentation. With the new letters they will practise blending for reading and will work on the high frequency words **no**, **go** and **I**. They will learn about the word endings **ff**, **ll** and **ss**.

When learning the process of blending for reading your child will be shown short words with 'sound buttons' under each letter sound. Each button (a dot for a single letter or a line for two letters that make one sound) represents a sound in the word.

up
• •

it
• •

They will start with VC (Vowel, Consonant) words such as **it** and **up** and will hear the teacher 'sound-talk' then say each word. With practice, your child will begin to sound-talk and say each word. When they are gaining success, they will move on to CVC words.

cat
• • •

sock
• • —

handy tip

Although the word **sock** ends with two consonants these work together as one consonant phoneme and so the word is still considered to be a CVC word.

Week 6

In the final week of Phase Two, your child will revise all the letters and sounds that they have worked on. By now they are beginning to develop as readers with skills in using a phonic approach.

They will also be practising the process of segmentation, which they started in Week 3, for spelling VC and CVC words. Here they will make use of letter fans or 'phoneme frames' with magnetic letters on a magnetic whiteboard.

This is a two-phoneme frame

… and this is a three-phoneme frame.

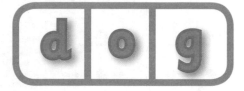

The teacher will say a VC word, such as **on** and then repeat it in sound-talk. She will then say a similar word, for example, **in**, and ask each child to say it in sound-talk to a partner. The group of children will continue to work on VC words with the teacher, finding the appropriate letters from a set of magnetic letters to place one at a time on the two-phoneme frame. VC words that can be used on the two-phoneme frame include: **on**, **in**, **an**, **it**, **at**, **up**.

Once the children are confident with VC words, they will move on to CVC words with the three-phoneme frame.

The children can also practise segmentation by using the letters on their letter fans. They can hold the letters so that only the two they need for a VC word are visible.

Your child will continue learning the 'tricky' high frequency words. The teacher may again show the children words with 'sound buttons':

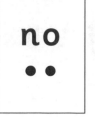
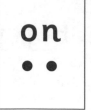

The teacher will sound-talk the words, showing the children that the letter **o** in the word **no** doesn't represent the same sound as it does in the word **on**. The word **no** may become the word of the day and will be shown to the children several times throughout the day. By the end of the day most children will be able to read the word without sounding it out.

Some words are especially tricky! Look at the word **the**:

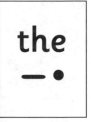

The word **the** is blended from the phonemes /**th**/, represented by the two letters **t** and **h**, and /**er**/, represented by just the letter **e**, so it is shown with a 'sound line' and a sound button. Again, the children will see this word repeatedly until they can recognise it confidently.

Your child will learn these other tricky high frequency words in the same way:

to I go into

By now, your child should have had so much practice with blending that they are able to read some of the other important high frequency words:

a an and as at

back big but can dad

get got had him

if in is it

mum not

of off

on put

up

What if my child is experiencing difficulties?

∗ Don't be surprised! This work is new for all the children at this stage and all of them will need plenty of practice.

∗ Go back a step or two. Revisit the work at Phase One, making sure that your child has lots of practice in all the aspects.

∗ Don't try to do too much at once. Practise just a small amount each day.

∗ Remember, your child will be busy all day at school and will be tired by the evening. They may be working perfectly well in lessons but may have had enough by the time you sit down to practise at home.

∗ Take the pressure off formal learning – enjoy sharing books together and don't expect your child to be reading them yet. Looking at the pictures and listening to you read will be giving your child valuable experience in preparation reading.

∗ Talk to the teacher and follow her advice. She knows the progress of all the children and will certainly know if your child is having any particular difficulty.

∗ Is there a possibility that your child might be having difficulty with hearing or sight? Even fluctuating hearing loss can affect a child's ability to discriminate sounds and can cause delays in learning. If you have any concerns, talk to your child's teacher or to your GP.

Phase Three takes place in the Reception class (ages four to five). During Phase Three your child will need to refer to the names of the letters as well as to the sounds that they make.

quick idea Help your child to learn the letter names (as opposed to the sounds) by singing an alphabet song together and pointing to the letters as you do so. Make sure that you separate out the letters clearly as you sing.

quick idea Point to each letter on pages 44 and 45, saying them to your child as you point. When you think they are ready, point to each letter and ask your child to tell you the name of that letter. When they are really confident, say 'find the letter **b**', 'find the letter **s**' and so on. Give lots of praise for success and lots of help if there is any difficulty. Remember your child will learn as much from mistakes as from successes.

Week 1

Your child will practise all the letters and sounds that they have already learnt and will learn this new set of letters:

j v w x

They will practise blending for reading and segmenting for spelling and they will read sentences, which include words using the letters they have learnt.

handy tip Never say 'You should know that already'!

u   c

                    m

d   v

      g   j   q

p

      e   l

                       z

      k   y

f

o

b

s

n

w

r

i

t

x

a

h

Week 2

Your child will practise all the letters and sounds that they have already learnt and will learn a new set of letters and sounds:

y   z   zz   qu

They will practise blending for reading and segmenting for spelling and they will read sentences, which include words using the letters they have learnt. They will be taught to read the tricky words **he** and **she** and they will be taught to spell the tricky words **the** and **to**, which they have already been learning to read.

Week 3

Your child will revise all the previous letters and sounds and will now learn some special consonant digraphs:

ch   sh   th   ng

They will be taught to read the tricky words **we**, **me** and **be** and will do lots of reading and spelling practice, including reading and writing captions and sentences.

A digraph is a group of two letters representing a single sound. Consonant digraphs are made up of consonant letters, not vowels.

Prepare five cards showing the words **he**, **she**, **we**, **me**, **be**. Ask your child to 'sound talk' each word by saying, for example, '**h–e**', and then to say the word, '**he**'. Make up a sentence that includes the word, such as 'He is a good boy.' Do this for each of the words then show the words to your child, asking them to say each word without sounding it out. Remember, practice makes perfect!

Weeks 8 to 10

During these weeks your child will practise blending for reading and segmenting for spelling. They will learn to read the tricky words **her**, **all** and **are**. They will practise reading and spelling two-syllable words and they will be extending the range of captions and sentences that they can both read and write. They will be taught to use capital letters at the start of sentences and full stops at the end.

Weeks 4 to 7

While continually revising all that they have previously learnt, your child will now be introduced to some vowel digraphs:

ai ee oa oo ar

or ur ow oi er

They will also meet some trigraphs:

ear air ure igh

The teacher will introduce the tricky words **was**, **my**, **you** and **they** for reading and will teach the spelling of the tricky words **no** and **go**.

handy tip A digraph is a group of two letters representing one sound and a trigraph has three letters representing one sound. A vowel digraph always starts with a vowel but its second letter could be a vowel or a consonant. For example, **oo** is a vowel digraph and so is **ow** (although it contains a consonant), because it makes an open sound like a vowel does.

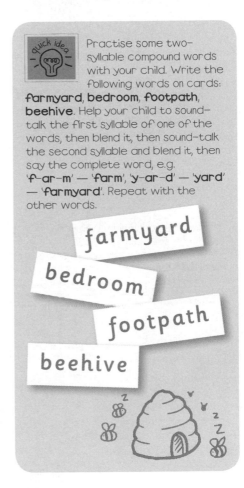

quick idea Practise some two-syllable compound words with your child. Write the following words on cards: **farmyard**, **bedroom**, **footpath**, **beehive**. Help your child to sound-talk the first syllable of one of the words, then blend it, then sound-talk the second syllable and blend it, then say the complete word, e.g. 'f-ar-m' — 'farm', 'y-ar-d' — 'yard' — 'farmyard'. Repeat with the other words.

farmyard

bedroom

footpath

beehive

Weeks 11 and 12

The final two weeks of Phase Three will be used for revision, if necessary, but if the children are ready they may move on to Phase Four.

What if my child is experiencing difficulties?

* Don't be surprised! This work is new for all the children at this stage and they will all need lots of practice.

* Revisit the activities for Phases One and Two, making sure that your child has lots of practice in all the aspects.

* Practise the names of the alphabet letters.

* Practise all the graphemes and phonemes that your child has learnt so far. For example, the grapheme ch, which represents the sound /**ch**/.

* Don't do too much at once. Practise just a small amount every day.

* Remember, your child will be busy all day at school and might be tired by the evening. They might be working perfectly well in lessons but have had enough by the time you sit down to practise at home.

* Continue to enjoy sharing books together, looking at the pictures and reading the words so that your child is hearing the sounds clearly and regularly.

* Talk to your child's teacher and follow her advice. She knows the progress of all the children and will certainly know if your child is having any particular difficulty.

* Is there a possibility that your child might be having difficulty with hearing or sight? Even fluctuating hearing loss can affect a child's ability to discriminate sounds and can cause delays in learning. If you have any concerns, talk to your child's teacher or to your GP.

Phase Four takes place in the Reception class (ages four to five). In this phase your child will consolidate their knowledge of words containing consonants that are next to each other. For example, words such as **lamp**, **tent** and **pond** each end with two consonants **mp**, **nt** and **nd.** By now, your child may have gained so much confidence that they can recognise some words instantly and can decode others very quickly. Throughout the four to six weeks of Phase Four, there will be lots of practice in reading and spelling high frequency words and in reading and writing complete sentences.

Week 1

Your child will learn to read and spell CVCC (Consonant, Vowel, Consonant, Consonant) words, such as: **sand**, **lamp**, **bent**, **melt**, **kept**, **vest**, **left**, **milk**.

quick idea

Write the words **sand**, lamp, bent, melt, kept, vest, **left** and milk on separate cards. Sound-talk each word then say each word with your child, for example, 's-a-n-d', 'sand'. Can your child read each of the words? If not, don't worry, practise again another day.

handy tip

Note that words such as **cart** or **hurt** are not considered as CVCC words because they consist of only three phonemes rather than four. The word cart has the central vowel phoneme /**ar**/ and the word hurt has the central vowel phoneme /**ur**/.

During this first week of Phase Four your child will learn to read the tricky words **said** and **so** and they will learn to spell **he**, **she**, **we**, **me** and **be**.

sand

lamp

bent

melt

kept

vest

left

milk

Week 2

As well as revising all their previous work, your child will learn to read and spell CCVC words (Consonant, Consonant, Vowel, Consonant), such as : **spot**, **blob**, **skin**, **smug**, **snug**, **grin**, **stop**, **swim**.

 Write the words **spot**, **blob**, **skin**, **smug**, **snug**, **grin**, **stop** and **swim** on separate cards. Sound-talk each word then say each word with your child, for example 's–p–o–t', 'spot'. Can your child read each of the words? If not, don't worry, practise again another day.

Your child will learn to read the tricky words **have**, **like**, **some**, **come** and they will learn to spell **was** and **you**. They will also read and spell some of the decodable high frequency words and they will be reading and writing sentences.

Week 3

Your child will practise reading and spelling more CVCC and CCVC words. They will learn to read the tricky words **were**, **there**, **little** and **one** and learn to spell the tricky words **they**, **all** and **are**.

handy tip

In school, your child will learn to read words before they learn to spell them. For example, they will have learnt to read **they**, **all** and **are** during Phase 3 and now, several weeks later, they will learn to spell these words in Phase 4.

Week 4

As well as practising the reading and spelling of more CVCC and CCVC words, your child will learn to read the tricky words **do**, **when**, **out** and **what** and to spell **my** and **her**.

CVCC words to practise at home

Help your child to read these words. It's best if you just practise five or six at a time. Later, you may like to use them for spelling practice.

Note that endings such as **ck** and **ss** are each considered to be a single consonant.

belt	band	best	camp
cold	cost	damp	dust
fold	fast	fist	gold
hold	help	hand	just
jump	lamp	lump	last
lost	mend	mast	must
nest	next	pest	post
pump	rest	ramp	sand
tent	vest	west	

bran   brick   clock   clam

clip-clop   drum   fan   flip

flop   flip-flop   flick   from

frog   grin   grab

pram   prod   plug   plan

plot   press   stop   step

stag   skip   skin   slip

slab   spot   spin   swim

trip   twin

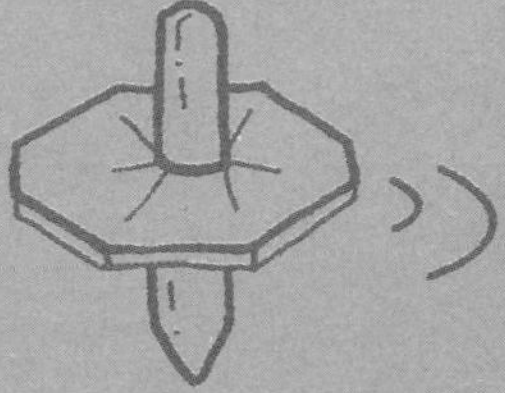

Segmenting for spelling

At school your child is likely to use magnetic letters with a phoneme frame. This time, they will use a four-phoneme frame.

Your child's teacher will say a CVCC word, such as **camp**, then say it in sound-talk. She is likely to stress the /**m**/. She will then repeat the process with another word, such as **melt**.

Now she will say another CVCC word but instead of saying it in sound-talk she will ask each child to sound-talk it to a partner. When all the children are ready the teacher will ask them to say which letters should be put in the phoneme frame. The children may also make the word on their letter-fan or on their own phoneme frame. They will repeat the process with more words.

The teacher will use the same process with CCVC words, but this time she will stress the second phoneme. For example, with the word **stop** she will stress the /**t**/.

The children may move on to learning to read and to spell CCVCC, CCCVC and CCCVCC words, such as **stamp**, **strum** and **stretch**. When segmenting for spelling these they will use five-phoneme or six-phoneme frames.

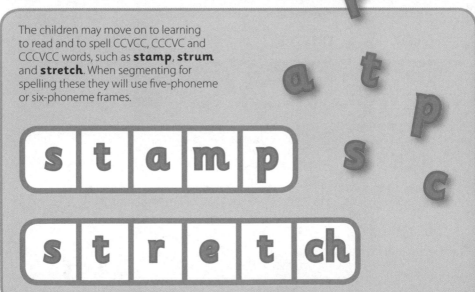

CCVCC words to practise at home

Help your child to read these words. It's best if you just practise five or six at a time. Later, you may like to use them for spelling practice. Note that endings such as **/ck/** and **/ss/** are each considered to be a single consonant phoneme.

blink

spend

frost

stamp

cramp

clamp

drink

crest

clasp

crisp

print

stand

plant

blank

grand

twist

grunt

tramp

blast

CCCVC words to practise at home

Note that /**ee**/ is considered to be a single vowel phoneme and /**ng**/ and /**ch**/ are considered to be single consonant phonemes.

CCCVCC words to practise at home

Note that the words stretch and scratch both feature the tch ending, which represents the phonemes /**t**/ and /**ch**/. It's interesting to consider whether we can actually hear any sound difference between the ending **ch** in words like **much** and the ending **tch** in words such as **match**.

What if my child is experiencing difficulties?

* Revisit the work at Phases Two and Three, making sure that your child has plenty of practice of all the graphemes and phonemes that they have learnt so far.

* Practise the names of the alphabet letters.

* Go back over the practice activities for Phase Four. Try to make these fun for your child, giving them lots of praise for success and lots of help where there is any difficulty.

* Don't do too much at once. Practise just a small amount each day.

* Remember, your child will be busy all day at school and might be tired by the evening. They may be working perfectly well in lessons but have had enough by the time you sit down to practise with them at home.

* Continue to enjoy sharing books together, looking at the pictures and reading the words so that your child is hearing the sounds clearly and regularly. Encourage your child to join in with your reading or to read aloud to you but only if they are happy to do so.

* Give lots of praise for success and try not to let your child feel under pressure.

* Talk to your child's teacher and follow her advice. She knows the progress of all the children and will certainly know if your child is having any particular difficulty.

* Is there a possibility that your child might be having difficulty with hearing or sight? Even fluctuating hearing loss can affect a child's ability to discriminate sounds and can cause delays in learning. If you have any concerns, talk to your child's teacher or to your GP.

Phase Five takes place throughout Year 1 (ages five to six). By the time your child enters this phase they will be able to read and spell a wide variety of words, including those that contain consonants that are next to each other. They will also have some experience of reading and spelling some words with more than one syllable.

At this stage your child will meet new graphemes that represent phonemes (sounds) they have already encountered with different graphemes. For example, they will have come across the grapheme **ai**, which can represent the phoneme /**ae**/ as in the word **rain**. Now, they will learn the graphemes **ay**, as in the word **day**, and **a-e** as in the word **late**. For some children this phase can be very challenging and they will need lots of practice with help from their teachers and parents.

Throughout this phase your child will practise reading and spelling high frequency words and words with more than one syllable. They will also practise reading and writing complete sentences.

Weeks 1 to 4

Each week your child will learn four new graphemes for reading. For example, **ou** as in **out**, **ea** as in **read**, **oy** as in **boy** and **ir** as in **girl**.

At some point during these four weeks they will also be taught a new phoneme /**zh**/ as in the words **measure** or **treasure**.

Your child will be taught to read **oh, their, people, Mr, Mrs, looked, called** and **asked**.

They will be taught to spell words that they have previously learnt to read:

said	so	have
like	come	were
there		

Weeks 5 to 7

Each week your child will be taught four alternative pronunciations of graphemes for reading. For example, they will be shown that the grapheme **a** can represent the phoneme /**a**/ as in **cat**, /**ae**/ as in **baby** and /**o**/ as in **was**. For people living in the South of England, the grapheme **a** can also represent the phoneme /**ar**/ as in **bath**!

Your child's teacher will teach them how to read the words:

water	where	who
again	thought	through
work	mouse	many
laughed	because	different
any	eyes	friends
once	please	

The children will also be taught the spelling of:

little	one	do
when	what	out

Weeks 8 to 30

Throughout this long period of time your child will consolidate their knowledge of letters and sounds. They will learn different pronunciations of graphemes and different spellings of phonemes. They will keep practising reading and spelling high-frequency words and words with more than one syllable. They will practise reading and writing full sentences. Their teacher will show them how to spell the words:

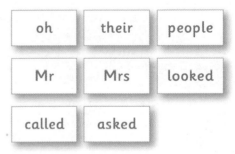

oh	their	people
Mr	Mrs	looked
called	asked	

quick idea Write these words on pieces of card. Pick three cards at random each day and practise reading them with your child. Practise together 'little but often'.

water	where	who
again	thought	through
work	mouse	many	laughed	because
please	different	any	eyes	friends	once

Words for reading practice

In Phase 5 your child will learn new graphemes for reading. For each grapheme we show a list of words that could be used for reading practice at home. Help your child to sound-talk each word, ensuring that they sound-talk each phoneme rather than each letter. For example, the word **out** would be sound-talked as /**ow**/-/**t**/.

handy tip

It's not a good idea to work through all the lists at once. Try practising one set of words each week over several weeks.

Grapheme ay representing the phoneme /ae/

day	may
play	say
way	stay
away	tray

Grapheme ou representing the phoneme /ow/

out	shout
about	mouse
house	found
round	loud

Grapheme ie representing the phoneme /ie/

tie	tied
pie	cried
lie	fried
lied	

Grapheme ea representing the phoneme /ee/

sea	read
eat	steam
seat	stream
beat	

Grapheme oy representing the phoneme /oi/

boy	royal
toy	annoy
enjoy	

Grapheme oe representing the phoneme /oe/

toe
goes
hoe

Help your child to sound-talk each word, ensuring that they sound-talk each phoneme rather than each letter. For example, the word **girl** would be sound-talked as /**g**/-/**ur**/-/**l**/.

Practise one set of words each week over several weeks.

Grapheme **ir** representing the phoneme /**ur**/

girl	first
bird	birthday
shirt	
thirsty	

Grapheme **aw** representing the phoneme /**or**/

saw	yawn
draw	awful
lawn	
drawn	

Grapheme **ue** representing the phoneme /**ue**/

*(note that this phoneme is sometimes shown as /**oo**/)*

glue	argue
blue	rescue
true	

Grapheme **ew** representing the phoneme /**oo**/

chew	screw
blew	flew
crew	

Grapheme **ew** representing the blended phonemes /**y**/ and /**ue**/ in some regions of the UK.

new	stew
few	knew

*Note the 'unsounded' letter **k**.*

Grapheme **ey** representing the phoneme /**ee**/

key	honey
money	chimney
monkey	
donkey	

Grapheme **au** representing the phoneme /**or**/

Paul

August

launch

automatic

*Automatic seems a very long word to be practising but it is decodable using phonic skills once the child knows that the grapheme **au** is representing /**or**/.*

Words for reading practice

Help your child to sound-talk each word, ensuring that they sound-talk each phoneme rather than each letter. For example, the word **came** would be sound-talked as /**k**/-/**ae**/-/**m**/.

Note that each grapheme on this page represents a 'split digraph'. A digraph is a group of two letters representing a single sound. A split digraph consists of two vowels separated by a consonant to make one phoneme.

Grapheme **a-e** representing the phoneme /**ae**/

came	take
made	cake
make	frame
place	late
shade	

Grapheme **e-e** representing the phoneme /**ee**/

these	Steve
athlete	Pete
Japanese	
Eve	

Grapheme **i-e** representing the phoneme /**ie**/

like	ice
liked	price
time	inside
slide	white

*Note that white starts with a new grapheme: wh representing the phoneme /**w**/.*

Grapheme **o-e** representing the phoneme /**oe**/

home	hole
alone	woke
globe	hope
note	chose
joke	

Grapheme **u-e** representing the phoneme /**ue**/
*(note that this phoneme is sometimes shown as /**oo**/)*

rude	costume
rule	tune
cute	June

Grapheme **u-e** representing the blended phonemes /**y**/ and /**ue**/ in some regions of the UK.

huge	amuse
cube	computer
tube	
use	

Help your child to sound-talk each word, ensuring that they sound-talk each phoneme rather than each letter. For example, the word **wheel** would be sound-talked as /**w**/-/**ee**/-/**l**/.

Practise one set of words each week over several weeks.

Note that both graphemes below represent consonant phonemes.

Grapheme **wh** representing the phoneme /**w**/

when	wheel
what	whisper
which	
where	
why	

Grapheme **ph** representing the phoneme /**f**/

phone	elephant
photo	alphabet
photograph	
dolphin	

Grapheme **wh** representing the phoneme /**h**/

who	whole
whose	

You may like to explain to your child that the letter **w** *is 'unsounded' in these words.*

Notice as well that in the words **who** *and* **whose** *the grapheme* **o** *is representing the phoneme /**ue**/.*

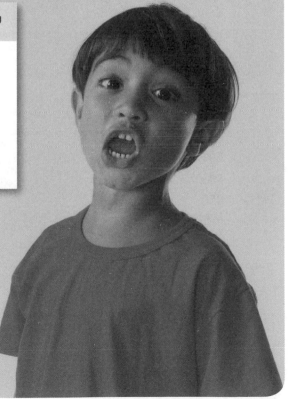

Words for reading practice

The words on this page feature different phonemes for specific graphemes. For example, the grapheme **a** can represent several different phonemes including /**a**/ as in **cat**, /**ae**/ as in **apron**, /**ar**/ as in **bath** (but note that this only applies in some southern regions of the UK), /**o**/ as in **was**.

Help your child to sound-talk each word, ensuring that they sound-talk each phoneme rather than each letter. For example, the word **able** would be sound-talked as /**ae**/-/**b**/-/**u**/-/**l**/.

The phoneme /**oo**/ can be heard in words such as **book** and **foot**. The phoneme /**ue**/ can be heard in words such as **soon** and **blue**.

Grapheme **a** representing the phoneme /**a**/	
and	**fast** (not Southern England)
hat	
had	**have**
man	**back**
that	**asked**

Grapheme **a** representing the phoneme /**ae**/	
acorn	apron
able	baby
table	lady
stable	angel
cable	

Grapheme **a** representing the phoneme /**ar**/ in southern regions of UK	
bath	**asked**
path	**can't** (most regions)
pass	
grass	**father** (most regions)
fast	

Grapheme **a** representing the phoneme /**o**/	
what	watch
was	wash
want	wasp

Grapheme **a** representing the phoneme /**e**/
any
many

The words on this page feature different phonemes for specific graphemes. For example, the grapheme **e** can represent different phonemes including /**e**/ as in bed and /**ee**/ as in **he**.

Help your child to sound-talk each word, ensuring that they sound-talk each phoneme rather than each letter. For example, the word **them** would be sound-talked as /**th**/-/**e**/-/**m**/.

Practise one set of words each week over several weeks. Most of the words in the lists below are within the lists of the top 300 most commonly used words and are therefore extremely important to every child learning to read.

Grapheme **e** representing the phoneme /**e**/

bed	never
then	next
them	tell
when	end
very	best
well	better
help	eggs
ever	

Grapheme **i** representing the phoneme /**i**/

his	going
with	thing
this	animal
little	fish
big	still
children	live
if	king
did	wish

Grapheme **e** representing the phoneme /**ee**/

he	she
we	even
me	Steven

Grapheme **i** representing the phoneme /**ie**/

find	wild
giant	child
I'm	kind
mind	behind

Words for reading practice

The words on this page feature different phonemes for specific graphemes. For example, the grapheme **o** can represent different phonemes including /**o**/ as in **dog** and /**oe**/ as in **go**.

Help your child to sound-talk each word, ensuring that they sound-talk each phoneme rather than each letter. For example, the word **clothes** would be sound-talked as /**k**/-/**l**/-/**oe**/-/**th**/-/**z**/.

Practise one set of words each week over several weeks. Most of the words in the lists below are within the lists of the top 300 most commonly used words and are therefore extremely important to every child learning to read.

Grapheme **o** representing the phoneme /**o**/	
of	dog
on	fox
not	stop
from	lots
off	hot
long	along

Grapheme **o** representing the phoneme /**oe**/	
no	going
don't	only
old	told
cold	clothes
hold	most
over	oh

Grapheme **u** representing the phoneme /**u**/	
hug	much
but	suddenly
mum	jump
just	run
us	under
must	sun

Grapheme **u** representing the phoneme /**ue**/ (note that this phoneme is sometimes shown as /**oo**/)
July
music
human
stupid

The words on this page feature different phonemes for specific graphemes. For example, the grapheme **ow** can represent different phonemes including **/ow/** as in **brown** and **/oe/** as in **snow**.

Help your child to sound-talk each word, ensuring that they sound-talk each phoneme rather than each letter. For example, the word **brown** would be sound-talked as **/b/-/r/-/ow/-/n/**.

Grapheme **ow** representing the phoneme **/ow/**

cow	owl
down	howl
now	town
how	
brown	
town	

Grapheme **ow** representing the phoneme **/oe/**

show	below
snow	window
blow	bowl
crow	**know** (Note the 'unsounded' letter **k**)
slow	
throw	grow

Grapheme **ie** representing the phoneme **/ie/**

pie	tied
tie	lied
lie	tried
tries	cried
cries	

Grapheme **ie** representing the phoneme **/ee/**

field	thief
piece	shriek
chief	

Grapheme **ie** representing the phoneme **/e/**

friend
friends

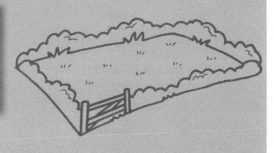

Words for reading practice

The words on this page feature different phonemes for specific graphemes. For example, the grapheme **ea** can represent different phonemes including /**ee**/ as in **tea** and /**e**/ as in **bread**.

Help your child to sound-talk each word, ensuring that they sound-talk each phoneme rather than each letter. For example, the word **bread** would be sound-talked as /**b**/-/**r**/-/**e**/-/**d**/.

Practise one set of words each week over several weeks. Most of the words in the lists below are within the lists of the top 300 most commonly used words and are therefore extremely important to every child learning to read.

Grapheme ea representing the phoneme /**ee**/

tea	team
really	east
please	cheap
sea	easy
leaf	eat
real	cheat
meal	clean
cream	mean
dream	read
scream	

Grapheme ea representing the phoneme /**e**/

bread	heavy
head	heaven
spread	ready
tread	already
thread	
ahead	
instead	
meant	
feather	
weather	

Grapheme ea representing the phoneme /**ae**/

great	break

Grapheme er representing the phoneme /**er**/

faster	never
water	mother
over	father
after	under
other	better
another	river

Grapheme er representing the phoneme /**ur**/

her	verse
herd	advert

The words on this page feature different phonemes for specific graphemes. For example, the grapheme **ou** can represent different phonemes including /**ow**/ as in found and /**ue**/ as in soup.

Help your child to sound-talk each word, ensuring that they sound-talk each phoneme rather than each letter. For example, the word **found** would be sound-talked as /**f**/-/**ow**/-/**n**/-/**d**/.

Grapheme **ou** representing the phoneme /**ow**/

out	round
found	around
sound	shout
ground	shouted
pound	cloud
about	count
house	amount
mouse	

Grapheme **ou** representing the phoneme /**ue**/ (note that this phoneme is sometimes shown as /**oo**/)

you
soup
group
route

Grapheme **ou** representing the phoneme /**oo**/

could
should
would
couldn't
shouldn't
wouldn't

Note the use of the apostrophe to replace the letter **o**.

Grapheme **ou** representing the phoneme /**oe**/

shoulder
boulder
mould
mouldy

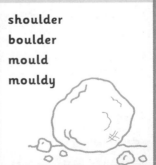

Words for reading practice

The words on this page feature different phonemes for specific graphemes. For example, the grapheme **y** can represent different phonemes including /**y**/ as in **yes** and /**ie**/ as in **by**.

Help your child to sound-talk each word, ensuring that they sound-talk each phoneme rather than each letter. For example, the word **why** would be sound-talked as /**w**/-/**ie**/.

Practise one set of words each week over several weeks. Most of the words in the lists below are within the lists of the top 300 most commonly used words and are therefore extremely important to every child learning to read.

Grapheme **y** representing the phoneme /**y**/

yes	yelp
yet	yesterday
yard	you
yell	York
yellow	

Grapheme **y** representing the phoneme /**ie**/

fly	spy
try	reply
cry	shy
sky	why
dry	July
pry	lullaby

Grapheme **y** representing the phoneme /**i**/

gym	mystery
crystal	bicycle

Grapheme **er** representing the phoneme /**ur**/

her	verse
herd	advert

Grapheme **y** representing the phoneme /**ee**/

very	really
baby	happy
lady	funny
every	carry
only	
many	
suddenly	
floppy	

What if my child is experiencing difficulties with reading?

It is not unusual for children to experience difficulties at Phase 5. During this phase they will be introduced to alternative graphemes to represent specific phonemes. For example, they will find out that the phoneme /**f**/ can be represented by the graphemes **f** or **ff** or **gh** (as in **laugh**) or **ph** (**photograph**). This is all tricky stuff!

They will also meet alternative phonemes represented by the same or similar graphemes. For example, look at these words: **cough**, **rough**, **through**, **thought**. Each of these words features the grapheme **ough**:

∗　In the word **cough**, the grapheme **ough** represents the blending of the phonemes /**o**/ and /**f**/.

∗　In the word **rough**, the grapheme **ough** represents the blending of the phonemes /**u**/ and /**f**/.

∗　In the word **through**, the grapheme **ough** represents just the phoneme /**ue**/ (note that this phoneme is sometimes shown /**oo**/).

∗　In the word **thought**, the grapheme **ough** represents just the phoneme /**or**/.

Look also at the grapheme **augh**. This can represent the blending of the phonemes /**a**/ and /**f**/ as in the word **laugh** (note that this word features the phonemes /**ar**/ and /**f**/ in the south of England), but it can also represent the phoneme /**or**/ as in **naughty** and **daughter**.

Is it surprising that some children find reading difficult? But with help and support they can make progress.

Handy tips

✱ Revisit the work at Phases Two, Three and Four, making sure that your child has lots of practice of all the graphemes and phonemes that they have learnt so far.

✱ Don't do too much at once. Practise just a small amount each day, giving lots of praise for success.

✱ Continue to enjoy sharing books together, looking at the pictures and reading the words so that your child is hearing the sounds clearly and regularly. Encourage your child to join in with your reading or to read aloud to you but only if they are happy to do so.

✱ Talk to your child's teacher and follow her advice. She knows the progress of all the children and will certainly know if your child is having any particular difficulty.

✱ Is there a possibility that your child might be having difficulty with hearing or sight? Even fluctuating hearing loss can affect a child's ability to discriminate sounds and can cause delays in learning. If you have any concerns, talk to your child's teacher or to your GP.

What if my child is making faster progress than others in the class?

You may be worried that your child is being held back by having to work at the same rate as others in the class. Your child may be making rapid progress with reading having developed skills in decoding text. You can help them to develop even further. They will benefit from hearing you read more difficult books aloud. Talk about the story, building up skills in comprehension (understanding of the story).

Words for spelling practice

For most children the process of learning to spell generally occurs later than reading. Pages 87 to 94 feature some lists of words that can be used for spelling practice. Below are some of the alternative spellings that can cause confusion for children when they are attempting to spell words containing particular phonemes. It is not advisable to work through these words at this stage but you should be aware that they may arise and know how to help your child if they do.

 handy tip

Your child may attempt to spell a word such as **adventure** by writing 'advencher'. Give them appropriate praise for doing so well but then point out that the last part is made of two sounds that can be shown in another way. Show them the complete word and help them to write it.

Phoneme	Common spellings	Alternatives
/ch/	**ch**in, **ch**ip, **ch**ur**ch**	pic**t**ure, adven**t**ure, ca**tch**, ki**tch**en
/j/	**j**am, **j**ar, **j**uice	he**dge**, ba**dge**
/m/	**m**ud, **m**ap, hi**m**	la**mb**, co**mb**, cli**mb**
/n/	**n**ext, **n**ot, **n**ew	**gn**at, **gn**ome, si**gn**, **kn**ock, **kn**ee, **kn**ot
/r/	**r**an, **r**ight, g**r**in	**wr**ap, **wr**ong, **wr**ite
/s/	**s**top, **s**aid, bu**s**	li**s**ten, ca**s**tle
/z/	**z**ip, **z**oo, fi**zz**	plea**se**, noi**se**, becau**se**
/i/	**i**n, **i**t, w**i**th	g**y**m, cr**y**stal, pr**e**tty, r**e**peat, plant**e**d, w**o**men
/ee/	s**ee**, tr**ee**, b**ee**n, n**ee**d	p**eo**ple, s**ea**, s**ea**t, r**ea**d, th**e**se, **e**ven, happ**y**, mumm**y**, dadd**y**, mon**ey**, hon**ey**, monk**ey**, f**ie**ld, sh**ie**ld, ch**ie**f
/ear/	**ear**, h**ear**, n**ear**	h**ere**, sph**ere**, ch**eer**, d**eer**, st**eer**
/ar/	c**ar**, g**ar**den, d**ar**k	b**a**th, gr**a**ss, **a**fter *(Southern England only)* f**a**ther, r**a**ther, h**a**lf, c**a**lf, p**a**lm

Phoneme	Common spellings	Alternatives
/air/	air, chair, pair	there, where, bear, wear, care, scare, stare, share
/or/	or, for, born	all, ball, talk, four, your, pour, ought, fought, thought, naughty, taught, daughter
/ur/	burn, turn	bird, girl, third, heard, learn, early word, world, work
/oo/	book, look, took, good	could, would, should, put, pull, full
/ai/	rain, train, main	day, play, tray, crayon, came, made, make, take
/ie/	pie, cried, tried	night, right, might, by, my, why, like, time, side, inside
/oa/	road, oats, soap	low, snow, slow, toe, hoe, home, over, clothes, woke, phone, old, cold, told, most

Phoneme	Common spellings	Alternatives
/y/-/ue/	due, statue, argue cube, tube, use, huge, tune, few, new	
/ue/ *(sometimes shown as /oo/ but this can cause confusion because /oo/ also represents the phoneme that appears in words such as look and book)*	moon, soon, school, food	blue, glue, true, June, rule, tune blew, grew, flew
/sh/	shop, push, rush	special, station, operation, action sure, sugar, chef, Charlotte
/zh/	usual, television, measure	

Phase Six takes place throughout Year 2 (ages six to seven). By now the children will know most of the common grapheme-phoneme correspondences, that is, the links between the letters and the sounds that they represent.

Linking letters and sounds

The children will be able to read a huge range of words at three levels:

1. decoding new words and speaking the sounds out loud as they do so

2. decoding words silently because they have the skills to sound and blend very quickly and effectively

3. reading words automatically because they know them already.

Reading to learn

The *Letters and Sounds* handbook that your child's teacher will be using now refers to children beginning the process of 'reading to learn' rather than 'learning to read'. Many children are at this stage, where they can read more and more texts independently.

It is very helpful for your child to experience a range of reading materials, both fiction and non-fiction. It is, of course, vital that they understand what they read. They may need help in making use of punctuation to help them understand the meaning.

Revisiting activities

Some children may not be so far advanced and should revisit the activities from previous phases. It is important that they sound-talk each word, sounding each phoneme rather than each letter. For example, the word **them** would be sound-talked as /**th**/-/**e**/-/**m**/ and not as /**t**/-/**h**/-/**e**/-/**m**/.

Spelling

Your child will extend their work in spelling and this, in turn, will help their reading.

The past tense

During Phase Six your child will be introduced to the idea of the past tense. They will experience activities where they hear sentences in the present tense and related sentences in the past tense. For example:

Today I am talking to my friends.

Yesterday I talked to my friends.

Today I am looking at some pictures.

Yesterday I looked at some pictures.

Talk to your child about things that happened yesterday. Try to use words in the simple past tense, rather than in the continuous past tense. For example, 'I baked some cookies yesterday' rather than 'I was baking some cookies yesterday'.

Your child will again use phoneme frames (see page 54) when working on adding the suffix **ed** to change some verbs to their past tense.

A suffix is an ending that's added to a word to make a new word, for example, want + ed = wanted, help + ful (the word 'full' is shortened to 'ful' when used as a suffix) = helpful.

At school your child will look at words such as:

look	⟶	looked
call	⟶	called
ask	⟶	asked
want	⟶	wanted
shout	⟶	shouted
need	⟶	needed
laugh	⟶	laughed
jump	⟶	jumped
pull	⟶	pulled
stop	⟶	stopped

Suffixes

Your child will learn about lots of suffixes and the rules for how they should be added to the ends of words to change meaning.

Suffix	Example	Notes
s	dog**s**, door**s**	
es	bus**es**, match**es**	The phonemes /e/ and /s/ are added to the **bus** and **match** when these words are made plural.
ed	jump**ed**, shopp**ed**, hop**ed**	The consonant **p** is doubled when the suffix **ed** is added to **shop**; the final **e** is dropped from the word **hope** when **ed** is added.
ing	jump**ing**, shopp**ing**	The consonant **p** is doubled when the suffix **ing** is added to **shop**.
ful	care**ful**, hope**ful**	
er	runn**er**, bigg**er**	The consonant **n** is doubled when the suffix **er** is added to **run**.
est	small**est**, bigg**est**, happi**est**	The consonant **g** is doubled when the suffix **est** is added to **big**; the **y** is replaced by a letter **i** when the suffix **est** is added to **happy**.
ly	bad**ly**, dark**ly**, happi**ly**	The **y** is replaced by a letter **i** when the suffix **ly** is added to **happy**.
ment	excite**ment**	
ness	dark**ness**, happi**ness**	The **y** is replaced by a letter **i** when the suffix **ness** is added to **happy**.
y	funn**y**, runn**y**, wind**y**	The consonant **n** is doubled when the suffix **y** is added to **fun** but nothing is added to **wind** as it already has two consonants before the **y** is added.

Vocabulary work

Your child will be introduced to lots of words to widen their vocabulary and they will be taught four memory strategies for learning the spellings of these words.

Four memory strategies

① Syllables

Listen to how many syllables (beats) the word has. Break the word into the syllables so that there are smaller parts to learn:

yesterday can be split into **yes-ter-day**

holiday can be split into **hol-i-day**

afternoon can be split into **af-ter-noon**

② Base words

Some longer words are built from 'base words':

Swimming is built from the base word **swim**, with the suffix **ing** added. It follows the rule that the consonant at the end of the base word has to be doubled.

③ Analogy

Some words are similar to others already known:

Could, **would** and **should** are similar to each other.

Couldn't, **wouldn't** and **shouldn't** are similar to each other.

④ Mnemonics

Some children enjoy using sentences to give a clue for the spelling of a word e.g. **because**:

Big **e**lephants **c**an **a**lways **u**nderstand **s**mall **e**lephants.

Big elephants can always understand small elephants!

79

Using sentences

Target words

Your child's teacher will give them whole sentences to learn in which the target words are featured. This not only ensures that your child is learning the words in context but also helps them to learn the process of punctuation.

Having introduced a set of words to the children, the teacher may dictate a sentence that includes several of the target words. The teacher will break the sentence into shorter phrases, repeating them several times while the children write them.

For example, to learn five of the high frequency words the children may follow this system:

1 Revise the five words by looking at them carefully and writing them down:

there   went   some   when   children

2 Look at and learn any extra words that may present difficulty in the sentence:

they   writing   school

3 Write the words within a sentence, listening to the sentence dictated by the teacher:

When the children went to school they did some writing there.

4 The sentence may be split into phrases, each of which will be repeated several times:

When the children ... went to school ... they did some writing there.

5 The children will check the sentence with a partner, comparing the writing to the words that the teacher now displays.

The same system will be used for other words that the children are focusing on.

Learning in different subjects

Over the course of Phase 6 your child will be writing more and more when learning about subjects such as history and science. The teacher will be marking their work and analysing any errors so that they can teach appropriately and set achievable targets for spelling.

handy tip

Ask your child's teacher if you can see their spelling targets. There may be a spelling log showing progress and targets.

$M = 5.9736 \times 10^{24} \text{ kg}$

$E = MC^2$

H_2O

$V_f = V_i + at$

$a^2 + b^2 = c^2$ x

$\pi = 3.14159265$

4cm

5cm

90°

$w = mg$

Method for learning difficult words

When your child has particularly difficult words to learn, the teacher may encourage them to follow this approach:

✓ Copy out the word on a card.

✓ Read the word aloud then turn the card over.

✓ Write out the word, saying the name of each letter.

✓ Read the word aloud.

✓ Turn the card back over and check.

✓ Correct any errors.

✓ Repeat the whole process three times.

✓ Do this every day for at least a week.

quick idea

Choose one of the word lists from pages 87 to 94. Follow the procedure shown above for each of the words on the list. Help your child to notice any spelling patterns that appear in the words.

Handwriting

Good, clear handwriting is essential for the development of effective spelling. Your child needs to be able to write each letter clearly and correctly. Ask your teacher to show you the school's handwriting policy.

Each letter should be formed as follows:

m n o

p q r

s t u

v w x

y z

83

Handwriting

Your child may already be using joined handwriting in school but it is important that you know how this handwriting is taught.

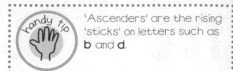

handy tip

'Ascenders' are the rising 'sticks' on letters such as **b** and **d**.

There are four basic joins:

1 slope joins to letters without ascenders:

an en in do um

2 bridge joins to letters without ascenders:

on ri vo wa fi

3 slope joins to letters with ascenders:

al eb it mb uh

4 bridge joins to letters with ascenders:

oh wh rl ot

Ask your child's teacher to show you the school's handwriting policy. Many schools will encourage the children **not** to join to or from some or all of the following letters:

b g j k p q s x y z

six

bags

jelly

foxes

keys

pin

quiz

zoo

Word lists for spelling practice

Use these lists of words for some fun spelling practice with your child.

Write out each list on a large sheet of paper. Make sure that you use the correct letter formation and the correct joins in accordance with the school's handwriting policy.

Talk about each word on the list. If any of the words are new to your child, try to make up a sentence that includes the word. Say the word, say the sentence, then say the word again. You may like to sound-talk each word, sounding each phoneme rather than each letter. For example, the word **ship** would be sound-talked as /**sh**/-/**i**/-/**p**/ and not as /**s**/-/**h**/-/**i**/-/**p**/.

Dictate the list of words to your child, giving them plenty of time to write the words down. Say the words as many times as they need. Ask your child to compare their words with the correct spellings of the words on your sheet of paper. Give lots of praise for successful spellings and help where there are any mistakes. Discuss these mistakes and compare the attempts with the correct spellings. Don't spend too long looking at the errors, as you want your child to remember the correct spellings not the incorrect ones!

Best success comes from short, regular fun practice rather than from long sessions of hard work. If your child wants to, however, you could extend the activity by asking them to write a full sentence that includes one of the words from the list.

When writing a sentence does your child remember to use a capital letter at the start and a full stop at the end? Encourage them to use a clear dot rather than a large blob as a full stop!

Word lists for spelling practice and for writing out in best handwriting.

sat	sad	pin
cat	had	tin
hat	dad	bin
van	bad	sit
can	ram	his
ran	Sam	him

hot	cup	sack
got	mum	lock
pot	put	neck
top	but	back
dot	run	lick
dog	cut	luck

bed	miss	hill
get	kiss	pull
ten	mess	bell
net	off	will
wet	huff	bull
red	fuss	sell

all	tall
ball	wall
call	hall

*Note that these words include the double **l** but also the letter **a** representing the phoneme /or/.*

jar	six
jam	box
Jack	fox
Jess	yet
jot	yes
jig	yap

zoo
zip
buzz
quiz
quick
quack

chin
chip
chop
chap
much
such

shop
ship
shout
ash
rush
rash

this
that
the
them
with
then

path   thick
bath   think
thin   thing

*Compare the sound made by the grapheme **th** in these words to the sound made by the same grapheme in the previous list.*

sing
song
long
king
bang
rang

black
blow
blush
brick
bring
brown

crack
crab
crust
dress
drip
drum

flag
flip
flop
fry
from
frost

glass
glad
grow
pram
plan
play

scrap
scrub
scan
skip
skin
skirt

sleep
slug
slip
spade
spot
spoon

small
smell
smile
sniff
snow
snap

splash
spring
swim
swing
square
squash

tree
train
trip
trap
tractor
try

cold
gold
wild
child
belt
help

hand
sand
kind
find
pond
fond

milk half
silk palm
calf calm

*Note that in the final four words on this list the phoneme /**ar**/ is represented by the grapheme **al**.*

camp
lamp
jump
stamp
pink
drink

lunch
bunch
munch
crunch
branch
bench

dust
just
list
last
must
pest

sweet
street
meet
feet
been
seen

sea
seat
beat
treat
read
tea

rain main
pain stain
train Spain

Encourage your child to use a capital letter at the start of any name of a person or place.

name	play	nice	school
came	stay	mice	food
same	away	twice	soon
make	spray	like	room
made	stray	time	moon
snake	may	inside	mood

coat	hope	book	looking
boat	rope	look	cook
home	soap	looked	good

*Your child may need help to distinguish between the words spelt with the grapheme **oa** and those spelt with the split digraph **o-e**, both representing the phoneme /**oe**/.*

*Although these words all feature the grapheme **oo**, the sound represented by this grapheme is not the same as the sound represented by the same grapheme in the list above.*

coin	owl	mouse
noise	town	house
noisy	flower	shout
voice	shower	about
spoil	tower	round
oil	power	found

hair	born	door
chair	sport	floor
stairs	morning	poor
fair		
pair	more	
repair	store	

*Your child may need help to distinguish between the words spelt with the grapheme **or** and those spelt with **oor**, both representing the phoneme /**or**/.*

more
store
snore
before
explore
core

bird	ear	head
girl	hear	bread
thirty	appear	feather
thirsty	near	weather
thirteen	clear	ready
shirt	disappear	instead

13

14

one	seven	thirteen
two	eight	fourteen
three	nine	fifteen
four	ten	sixteen
five	eleven	seventeen
six	twelve	eighteen

15

16

Monday	Friday	January	July
Tuesday	Saturday	February	August
Wednesday	Sunday	March	September
Thursday		April	October
		May	November
		June	December

Remind your child that days of the week and months of the year start with capital letters.

helped	stopped slipped	laughed parked
looked	hopped hummed	lived talked
called	shopped pegged	jumped walked
asked		
wanted	*For each word, encourage your child to think about the 'base word' to which the suffix **ed** has been added.*	*The end letter **e** has been removed from the word **live** before the suffix **ed** has been added.*
shouted		

swimming	sitting
shopping	skipping
running	stepping

*For each word, encourage your child to think about the 'base word' to which the suffix **ing** has been added.*

hoping	taking
coming	caring
smiling	making

*Each of the base words features a vowel, then a consonant, then the letter **e**. For example, **hope**. The end letter **e** has been removed from each base word before the suffix **ing** has been added.*

puzzle
paddle
giggle
rattle
nibble
fiddle

puzzling	rattling
paddling	nibbling
giggling	fiddling

*Each base word features a double consonant then **le**. The end letter **e** has been removed from each base word before the suffix **ing** has been added.*

tickle
trickle
crackle
chuckle
tackle
prickle

tickling	chuckling
trickling	tackling
crackling	prickling

*Each base word features two consonants then **le**. The end letter **e** has been removed from each base word before the suffix **ing** has been added.*

agree
appear
like
write
cycle
place

disagree   rewrite
disappear   recycle
dislike   replace

*The prefixes **dis** and **re** have been added to the base words on the previous list.*

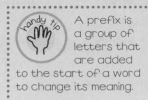

A prefix is a group of letters that are added to the start of a word to change its meaning.

---

fast   quick
faster   quicker
fastest   quickest

*The suffixes **er** and **est** are added to the base words fast and quick. Can your child think of other similar words?*

happy   happiness
silly   silliness
crazy   craziness

*The final letter **y** is replaced by a letter **i** when the suffix is added.*

---

bigger   biggest
fitter   fittest
sadder   saddest

*Does your child notice that each of the base words ends with a single consonant but that this is doubled when the suffix is added? For example, **big** ends with a single **g**.*

fun   sunny
funny   sunnier
funnier   sunniest
funniest

*The consonant **n** is doubled in the base word **fun** when the suffix **y** is added. This final **y** is replaced by an **i** when a further suffix is added.*

boys	chairs
girls	books
tables	doors

*To make each word plural, the letter **s** is added to the base word.*

catches	brushes
matches	foxes
wishes	boxes

*To make each word plural, the letters **es** are added to the base word. The new word has two syllables (beats).*

days	donkeys
keys	monkeys
trays	holidays

*Words that end with a vowel then **y**, usually just need the letter **s** to make them plural.*

babies	puppies
ladies	parties
ponies	lollies

*Where words end with a consonant then **y**, the **y** is replaced by **i** before the **es** is added.*

wolf	wolves
calf	calves
knife	knives

*Some words that end with letter **f** need to have a **v** in place of the **f** when they become plural. Note that the phoneme /**n**/ is represented by the grapheme **kn** in the final two words.*

playground	weekend
motorway	pancake
bedroom	downstairs

These words are all 'compound' words, each made from the combination of two shorter words.

Useful information

Phoneme

A phoneme is a unit of sound and can be represented by:

- one letter, for example, **b** as in **b**at
- two letters, for example, **ee** as in sw**ee**t
- three letters, for example, **ear** as in n**ear**

Note that a phoneme (a sound) can be represented in several ways. For example, the sound ee can be represented by:

/**ee**/ as in f**ee**t

/**ei**/ as in c**ei**ling

/**ie**/ as in ch**ie**f

/**ea**/ as in n**ea**t

/**i**/ as in sk**i**

/**e_e**/ as in P**e**t**e**

Vowel phoneme

A vowel phoneme makes an open sound and always contains at least one vowel – you usually have to open your mouth to say it. For example:

/**a**/ as in b**a**t

/**ie**/ as in cr**ie**s

/**oo**/ as in b**oo**k

/**ur**/ as in t**ur**n

/**ow**/ as in t**ow**n

Consonant phoneme

A consonant phoneme always contains at least one consonant and usually involves closing the mouth, or 'biting' the lower lip, or touching the roof of the mouth with the tongue. (There are exceptions, for example, h.)

/**b**/ as in **b**at

/**f**/ as in **ph**otogra**ph**

/**th**/ as in **th**ey

/**ng**/ as in si**ng**

Grapheme

A grapheme is a letter or pair of letters or group of letters representing a single sound. For example, **ee**, **ei**, **ie**, **ea**, **i** and **e_e** are all graphemes representing the sound ee.

Digraph

A digraph is a group of two letters representing a single sound. So, for example, the grapheme **ch** is a consonant digraph because it is made up of two consonants. The grapheme **ee** is a vowel digraph but **ow** is also a vowel digraph, although it contains a consonant, because it makes an open sound like a vowel does.

Split digraph

A split digraph consists of two vowels separated by a consonant to make one phoneme. For example:

e_e as in P**e**t**e**

i_e as in m**i**n**e**

a_e as in c**a**m**e**

Cluster

A cluster consists of two or three letters making more than one sound. For example:

t h r

are three letters that can make the cluster **thr**, which consists of the phonemes /**th**/ and /**r**/.

Blending

Blending is the process of combining different sounds (phonemes) to be able to say a particular word. For example:

/**sh**/ /**i**/ /**p**/

can be blended to make the word **ship**.

Segmenting

Segmenting is the process of splitting a word into its different phonemes to be able to spell the word. For example:

ship can be segmented into the phonemes /**sh**/ /**i**/ /**p**/.

VC

vowel/consonant, for example, the word **it**

CV

consonant/vowel, for example, the word **be**

CVC

consonant/vowel/consonant, for example, the word **cat**

CCVC

consonant/consonant/vowel/consonant, for example, the word **stop**

CVCC

consonant/vowel/consonant/consonant, for example, the word **fast**